Growing a
Heart for God

1 AND 2 SAMUEL

New Community Bible Study Series

Old Testament
  Exodus: Journey toward God
  1 and 2 Samuel: Growing a Heart for God
  Nehemiah: Overcoming Challenges
  Psalms Vol. 1: Encountering God
  Psalms Vol. 2: Life-Changing Lessons
  Daniel: Pursuing Integrity
New Testament
  Sermon on the Mount 1: Connect with God
  Sermon on the Mount 2: Connect with Others
  The Lord's Prayer: Praying with Power
  Parables: Imagine Life God's Way
  Luke: Lessons from Jesus
  Acts: Build Community
  Romans: Find Freedom
  2 Corinthians: Serving from the Heart
  Philippians: Run the Race
  Colossians: Discover the New You
  James: Live Wisely
  1 Peter: Stand Strong
  1 John: Love Each Other
  Revelation: Experience God's Power

JOHN ORTBERG

WITH KEVIN & SHERRY HARNEY

New Community
KNOWING. LOVING. SERVING. CELEBRATING.

Growing a
Heart for God

1 AND 2 SAMUEL

ZONDERVAN.com/
AUTHORTRACKER
follow your favorite authors

ZONDERVAN®

1 and 2 Samuel: Growing a Heart for God
Copyright © 2008 by Willow Creek Association

Requests for information should be addressed to:

Zondervan, *Grand Rapids, Michigan 49530*

ISBN 978-0-310-28049-1

Interior design by Sherri Hoffman

Printed in the United States of America

11 12 13 14 • 21 20 19 18 17 16 15 14 13 12 11 10 9 8 7 6 5 4 3 2

New Community Bible Study Series   6

Introduction   11

Session I

What Matters Most to God? The Heart! —
1 Samuel 16:1–13   13

Session 2

A Bold Heart — 1 Samuel 17:1–50   20

Session 3

Hope for a Discouraged Heart —
1 Samuel 18–24, 30   28

Session 4

A Contrite Heart — 2 Samuel 11–12   38

Session 5

A Broken Heart — 2 Samuel 13–18   47

Session 6

A Generous Heart —
1 Samuel 30; 2 Samuel 24   55

Leader's Notes   64

God has created us for community. This need is built into the very fiber of our being, the DNA of our spirit. As Christians, our deepest desire is to see the truth of God's Word as it influences our relationships with others. We long for a dynamic encounter with God's Word, intimate closeness with his people, and radical transformation of our lives. But how can we accomplish those three difficult tasks?

The New Community Bible Study Series creates a place for all of this to happen. In-depth Bible study, community-building opportunities, and life-changing applications are all built into every session of this small group study guide.

How to Build Community

How do we build a strong, healthy Christian community? The whole concept for this study grows out of a fundamental understanding of Christian community that is dynamic and transformational. We believe that Christians don't simply gather to exchange doctrinal affirmations. Rather, believers are called by God to get into each other's lives. We are family, for better or for worse, and we need to connect with each other.

Community is not built through sitting in the same building and singing the same songs. It is forged in the fires of life. When we know each other deeply—the good, the bad, and the ugly—community is experienced. Community grows when we learn to rejoice with one another, celebrating life. Roots grow deep when we know we are loved by others and are free to extend love to them as well. Finally, community deepens and is built when we commit to serve each other and let others serve us. This process of doing ministry and humbly receiving the ministry of others is critical for healthy community life.

Build Community Through Knowing and Being Known

We all long to know others deeply and to be fully known by them. Although we might run from this level of intimacy at times, we all want to have people in our lives who trust us enough to disclose the deep and tender parts of themselves. In turn, we want to reveal some of our feelings, expressing them freely to people we trust.

The first section of each of these six studies creates a place for deep knowing and being known. Through serious reflection on the truth of Scripture, you will be invited to communicate parts of your heart and life with your small group members. You might even discover yourself opening parts of your heart that you have thus far kept hidden. The Bible study and discussion questions do not encourage surface conversation. The only way to go deep in knowing others and being known by them is to dig deep, and this takes work. Knowing others also takes trust — that you will honor each other and respect each other's confidences.

Build Community Through Celebrating and Being Celebrated

If you have not had a good blush recently, read a short book in the Bible called Song of Songs. It's a record of a bride and groom writing poetic and romantic love letters to each other. They are freely celebrating every conceivable aspect of each other's personality, character, and physical appearance. At one point the groom says, "You have made my heart beat fast with a single glance from your eyes." Song of Songs is a reckless celebration of life, love, and all that is good.

We need to recapture the joy and freedom of celebration. In every session of this study, your group will commit to celebrate together. Although there are many ways to express joy, we will let our expression of celebration come through prayer. In each session you will take time to come before the God of joy and celebrate who he is and what he is doing. You will also have opportunity to celebrate what God is doing in your life and the lives of those who are a part of your small group. You will become a community of affirmation, celebration, and joy through your prayer time together.

You will need to be sensitive during this time of prayer together. Not everyone feels comfortable praying with a group of people. Be aware that each person is starting at a different place in their freedom to pray in a group, so be patient. Seek to promote a warm and welcoming atmosphere where each person can stretch a little and learn what it means to be a community that celebrates with God in the center.

Build Community Through Loving and Being Loved

Unless we are exchanging deeply committed levels of love with a few people, we will die slowly on the inside. This is precisely why so many people feel almost nothing at all. If we don't learn to exchange love with family and friends, we will eventually grow numb and no longer believe love is even a possibility. This is not God's plan. He hungers for us to be loved and to give love to others. As a matter of fact, he wants this for us even more than we want it for ourselves.

Every session in this study will address the area of loving and being loved. You will be challenged, in your personal life and as a small group, to be intentional and consistent about building loving relationships. You will get practical tools and be encouraged to set measurable goals for giving and receiving love.

Build Community Through Serving and Being Served

Community is about serving and humbly allowing others to serve you. The single most stirring example of this is recorded in John 13, where Jesus takes the position of the lowest servant and washes the feet of his followers. He gives them a powerful example and then calls them to follow. Servanthood is at the very core of community. To sustain deep relationships over a long period of time, there must be humility and a willingness to serve each other.

At the close of each session will be a clear challenge to servanthood. As a group, and as individual followers of Christ, you will discover that community is built through serving others. You will also find that your own small group members will grow in their ability to extend service to your life.

Bible Study Basics

To get the most out of this study, you will need to prepare and participate. Here are some guidelines to help you.

Preparing for the Study

1. If possible, even if you are not the leader, look over each session before you meet, read the Bible passages, and answer the questions. The more you are prepared, the more you will gain from the study.
2. Begin your preparation with prayer. Ask God to help you understand the passage and apply it to your life.
3. A good modern translation, such as the New International Version, Today's New International Version, the New American Standard Bible, or the New Revised Standard Version, will give you the most help. Questions in this guide are based on the New International Version.
4. Read and reread the passages. You must know what the passage says before you can understand what it means and how it applies to you.
5. Write your answers in the spaces provided in the study guide. This will help you participate more fully in the discussion and will also help you personalize what you are learning.
6. Keep a Bible dictionary handy to look up unfamiliar words, names, or places.

Participating in the Study

1. Be willing to join in the discussion. The leader of the group will not be lecturing but will encourage people to discuss what they have learned in the passage. Plan to share what God has taught you during your preparation time.
2. Stick to the passages being studied. Base your answers on the verses being discussed rather than on outside authorities such as commentaries or your favorite author or speaker.

3. Try to be sensitive to the other members of the group. Listen attentively when they speak, and be affirming whenever you can. This will encourage more hesistant members of the group to participate.
4. Be careful not to dominate the discussion. By all means participate, but allow others to have equal time.
5. If you are a discussion leader or a participant who wants further insights, you will find additional comments in the Leader's Notes at the back of the book.

1 and 2 Samuel: Growing a Heart for God

One scholar said if he had to name a single Renaissance man in human history, somebody with extraordinary capacities on multiple fronts, David would be at the top of the list.

He was a *musician* so skilled that a king would summon him to play because his music would drive away the king's depression when nothing else helped. David was the musical equivalent to Prozac.

He was a formidable *warrior* who won a legendary battle against a great champion when he wasn't even old enough to shave. He attracted the greatest soldiers of his day to serve under him, and he subjugated his nation's enemies in a way that Israel had never experienced before and would never experience again.

He was a fierce *competitor*. He'd take on a lion, a bear— anything—just name the challenge, and he was ready to face it.

He was a *poet*. He wrote psalms that expressed the deep longing of the human heart for God. His words were so personal and powerful that thousands of years later, they remain the single most moving and influential devotional literature ever written. David wrote the prayer book for the human race.

He was a *statesman*. He had such wisdom and political skill that Israel achieved its highest level of economic well-being and political stability under his reign. His kingship would forever be remembered as the golden age of Israel—his rule was seen as Israel's version of the idyllic Camelot. The time of David's rule would be locked so powerfully in the people's memories that they would refer to the Messiah as the "Son of David," because they hoped he would reclaim the glory that existed when David was on the throne.

David was also an immensely *attractive person*. We're told several times that he was attractive physically and in his personality.

Men and women alike were drawn to his charismatic presence. He was a magnetic figure.

All this in one man ... amazing!

David had the poetic soul of a Shakespeare, the competitive heart of a Tiger Woods, the musicianship of a Pavarotti, the statesmanship of a Lincoln, and the physical attractiveness of a Brad Pitt. This guy had the whole package!

In many ways, David was the central character of the Old Testament. Just look at the space devoted to him. Abraham has fourteen chapters about his life and Elijah has ten chapters that tell his story. David has about sixty-six chapters in Scripture devoted to him. He's mentioned about six hundred times in the Old Testament and another sixty times in the New Testament.

So exceptional is his memory that David is the final human character named in all of Scripture. In Revelation 22:16 Jesus says, "I am the Root and the Offspring of David, and the bright Morning Star." To this day, the flag that flies over Israel features the Star of David. He was a remarkable man.

In light of all his outward accomplishments, what God declared was most extraordinary about David, what drew God to him, was his *heart*. As much as all the things listed earlier are impressive to other human beings, God was far more interested in David's heart.

A close study of the life of David will open our eyes to how much God cares about the condition of *our* hearts. The world spends a lot of time pressing us to focus on exterior issues, but God looks on the inside. Over the course of these six sessions that grow out of 1–2 Samuel, we will discover that God cares more about the condition of our hearts than we ever dreamed. And we will learn to develop hearts that yearn for the heart of God.

What Matters Most to God? The Heart!

I SAMUEL 16:1 – 13

In recent years there has been a great deal written about birth order and how it impacts children and the way they grow up. This is nothing new ... there was a real big significance to the birth order in Old Testament times. In the Hebrew language, the term "youngest" meant not merely the last-born, but also the lowest in rank. Those who are not firstborn children can sometimes be heard commenting about how the firstborn has certain unfair advantages.

One example of this, as observed by Bill Butterworth, can show up in the family photo album. To paraphrase Bill, we might hear a parent say something like this as they open their family photo album, "Here is a picture of our firstborn, little Sally, the moment she entered this world. Here is a picture of Sally at two minutes old; here is another one at ten minutes. Oh, here is baby Sally taking her first nap, this is her first bath, and this is her first meal. Oh, here are some pictures of day two!" Then, the same parent continues, "Here are pictures of Timothy, our second-born. Here he is when he was born, here is his first smile, and here is his first birthday." Then, it comes time to show the pictures of the last-born: "Here is a picture of when little Danny was born, and here is his tenth birthday ... wow, we need to take more pictures of Danny!"

A fascinating thread runs through the Old Testament having to do with a *reversal of birth order* and the rights that normally came with being a firstborn son among the people of Israel. Ishmael was the first son born to Abraham, but God chose Isaac. Esau, a twin, came out of the womb first, but God decided to continue the line of the patriarchs through his younger twin brother Jacob. Jacob's son Joseph had ten older brothers, but God called Joseph to a role of leadership and authority in the family. David was the baby of the family and had seven older brothers, but he became the king of Israel.

What is God saying through these significant reversals: that firstborn kids are a bunch of spoiled brats and he likes middle or younger kids better? As a non-firstborn child, I have to give my unbiased opinion and say that's exactly the point. Not really! Something far more significant is going on here.

In those days, everything went to the firstborn—all rights, property, and privileges. That's the way the power structures worked at that time in history. But God is breaking into the ordinary cultural practices of human life and doing something new. Old limitations and boundaries about who counts and who doesn't don't apply anymore. He's not bound or beholden to any human system or power. His kingdom is going to shake some things up. In light of God's power at work in our lives and the world, birth order is really not that big of a deal.

Making the Connection

1. Where did you fall in your family's birth order and how has this impacted you?

Knowing and Being Known

Read I Samuel 16:1 – 13

2. Imagine you were a fly on the wall of Jesse's living room while this drama unfolds. What would you have learned about *one* of the following characters in the story?

- Jesse
- Samuel
- David
- God

A Wild Heart

David's heart was characterized by a sense of wild abandon. His heart was fully committed to God. In Psalm 9:1 David says, "I will praise you, O LORD, with all my heart; I will tell of all your wonders." That same passionate declaration occurs again in Psalms 86 and 111. David had an unguarded passion and heart, and he never held it back. He wasn't calculating and cautious with his heart. He was generous and free.

One morning I was driving to work and paused to observe some kids waiting for the school bus. Most of them were trying to look cool because there were other kids present. But this one little guy — I would guess he was about six years old — was standing a few feet apart from the others, so happy he was jumping up and down. He had a huge smile on his face and was just bouncing with joy. In a sad, sober mass of school-bound kids, this one child stood out among the rest. As I watched him I wanted to get out of my car and jump up and down with him. I thought, *It must make God happy when he sees his children so filled with joy and gratitude that they can't help but jump up and down.*

Read 2 Samuel 6:12 – 22

3. This passage depicts a vivid and dramatic contrast between King David and his wife Michal. How are their hearts different and how does this impact their actions?

4. Michal did not feel free to express herself with wild abandon and she tried to get David to settle down and be more dignified. What are some of the reasons that we might hold back and not let our hearts loose before God and others?

5. Everyone looks different when they celebrate and go wild for God. What do you look like when you are expressing your love and appreciation for God?

A Reflective Heart

David's heart was characterized by deep reflection. In one of David's psalms he writes, "Search me, O God, and know my heart; test me and know my anxious thoughts" (Psalm 139:23). It is a rare combination to find a person who is committed to passionate action on the one hand, and deep reflection on the other, but David was such a man. David's heart grew deep and reflective in all his years alone with God.

David spent much of his life waiting. When he was a kid, he tended sheep ... this provided lots of quiet time. Then there came this amazing day when the prophet Samuel arrived and anointed David as king. But David didn't just march into Jerusalem after this and sit on a throne. Saul was still king so David went back to the sheep ... and waited some more. But the years in the wilderness were not wasted ones. He was learning to be alone with God. He was growing deep.

Richard Foster wrote, "Superficiality is the curse of our age."

Richard Swenson said, "We're so bombarded with noise, the gift that most people need this Christmas is not a cordless phone, but a phone-less cord."

6. When you are running on the fast track of life and fail to make space for quiet reflection, how does this impact *one* of the following?
    • Your relationships with friends and family
    • Your attitude at work
    • Your outlook on the future
    • How you face times of conflict and tension
    • Your sense of intimacy with God

7. What are some of the things that can get in the way of our developing and maintaining a reflective heart?

8. David found space for deep reflection in the pastures with his small flock of sheep. What place or practices help you develop a reflective heart?

A Heart with Stubborn Love

David's heart was characterized, right down to the core, by stubborn love. In Psalm 78:72 we read that David shepherded the people with integrity of heart. The idea here is that his heart was undivided. It's the opposite of fickle. He loved people with the loyal heart of a shepherd who kept loving the sheep, even when they were obstinate.

Think about how David loved Saul, even when it was hard. King Saul became increasingly corrupt and tormented by pathological jealousy of David. Saul was constantly deceiving David and on several occasions he tried to kill him. What's most amazing is how, through it all, David loved him. Twice David could have killed Saul — and he would have been justified in the eyes of most people — but he refused to do it. When Saul finally died, David wrote one of the most beautiful poems ever written as a lament for him, "How the mighty have fallen!... O daughters of Israel, weep for Saul!" How could David find tears for a man like that? He knew all about Saul's faults, better than anybody, and he knew about Saul's possibilities, and he loved him to the end.

9. Tell about a person in your life who has exemplified stubborn love for you. How has their life taught you about the heart of God?

10. We all have relationships with people who have hurt and wronged us. Think of one person to whom you need to extend stubborn love and how you might do this in the coming weeks. (Share your thoughts without using the person's name.)

Celebrating and Being Celebrated

When was the last time you were so full of gratitude to God that you jumped up and down? When was a time when you just had to express your joy with some measure of wild abandon? Take a moment to write down a few things God has done or is doing in your life that cause you to celebrate his goodness.

Take a moment as a group to jump up and down together! You don't have to do this, literally, although you should feel free to if you would like. Read your list of good-God things and share joy together. Imagine God watching your group as you share, a loving Father who rejoices in our joy ... and dare to get a little reckless as you celebrate together.

Loving and Being Loved

At the end of Psalm 23, David declares, with a passionate heart, "I will dwell in the house of the LORD forever." He loved God with a stubborn love that would not relent. He didn't say, "I hope that I will dwell in the house of the Lord." He didn't say, "It may be that I'll dwell in the house."

David had the heart of a racehorse. He declared for all to hear, "I'm staying in the house. I know I make a mess sometimes, and I may spill on the rug, and knock down the lamps, and break all the expensive stuff. I know what a pain it is to have me in the house, but I'll tell you what: You're going to have to drag me out of here kicking and screaming. I will dwell in the house of the Lord forever." That was the heart of David and it can be our heart as well.

Take time as a group to pray together. Thank God for opening his house to you through the life, love, and sacrifice of Jesus. Thank God for loving you that much. Declare to God that you love him and that you will joyfully dwell in his house forever!

Serving and Being Served

There are times when we are called to serve others, and times we are invited to serve God. As you begin this series on the life of David, consider a simple act of worship that will serve God, yourself, and your small group. Take time in the coming weeks to read through the psalms David wrote. Just look at the superscription above each psalm and you will see if it is a psalm of David. Begin with Psalm 3, and read one or two of David's psalms each day. This process will give you insight into the heart of God, David, and your own heart.

A Bold Heart

I SAMUEL 17:1–50

Goliath would have been a very high draft pick in the NBA. He stood over nine feet tall. He was commonly referred to as "the champion of the Philistines." His armor, which covered him like a human tank, weighed about two hundred pounds. The head of his spear weighed twenty-five pounds ... imagine that flying at you. There is an old Jim Croce song that says, "You don't mess around with Jim." It would be easy to imagine a similar song back in David's day called, "You don't mess around with Goliath."

This war-machine of a man stood in front of God's people and made an offer. He invited any one man to walk out of the ranks of Israel's army and fight him one-on-one. The bet was simple. Winner takes all. Goliath made this offer for forty straight days. And, in response to his daily challenge, Goliath found no takers ... until day forty-one.

On the forty-first day of Goliath's taunt, a young boy with a heart as big as the Jordan River stepped out and accepted the offer ... a fight, to the death, against a giant. David exhibited a heart of boldness that stands as an example thousands of years later.

Each of us wants to live with a bold heart. We want to exhibit the kind of courage David did when he faced Goliath. But if we look carefully at David's story and life, we discover it takes time to grow a bold heart. David's boldness quotient was being built a long time before he met Goliath.

There is a real illusion today that when we face a moment of crisis, a "Goliath Moment," we can respond with a bold heart just out of the blue. But it doesn't happen that way. The truth is, if you wait until you're facing your "Goliath Moment" to become a bold person, you probably won't do too well.

A bold heart needs to grow a little stronger every day. This was true for David and it is true for each one of us. If we want to live with a bold heart, the time to begin exercising the trait of boldness is today.

Making the Connection

1. If you have faced a "Goliath Moment" in your life, what was it and how did you make it through?

Knowing and Being Known

Read 1 Samuel 17:1 – 27

2. Imagine yourself standing among the ranks of Israel's warriors during the forty days Goliath issued his challenge. What thoughts might be running through your mind? What is the condition and attitude of Israel's army?

Boldly Facing Everyday Challenges

Ordinary daily challenges provide an opportunity to develop a bold heart. The countless days and nights that David tended sheep became a laboratory for growing boldness. Sometimes we picture the life of a shepherd as only quiet hours watching the sheep graze. However, we must understand there was also the constant danger of wild animals pouncing on wayward sheep. Lions, bears, and other predators were always hunting for their next lunch. A shepherd had to be bold and ready to fight for the flock at all times. So, on many occasions, in the daily grind of David's work as a shepherd, he faced opportunities to protect his little flock.

In the same way, we grow a bold heart by standing strong in the countless moments of life that can pass almost unnoticed. Each time a parent loves a child enough to confront a negative attitude or behavior, boldness is growing. When a spouse scrutinizes their own words and admits they have been harsh or insensitive, their courage quotient increases. As a business person rejects an offer that is at all shady or questionable, they are fighting a battle that prepares them for a bigger victory in the future. When a man or woman overhears a juicy morsel of gossip and refuses to pass it on to anyone else, boldness is being fortified. It is the little decisions in daily life that prepare us for the "Goliath Moments."

Read 1 Samuel 17:32 – 37

3. What connections did David make between his daily work as a shepherd and his preparedness to face Goliath?

4. What is one daily challenge you face that could become a laboratory for God to grow boldness in your life? What is a small step of faithful boldness you can take in this area of your life?

How can your group members pray for you and keep you accountable as you seek to live with daily boldness in this area?

Boldly Facing Criticism and Opposition

David got hand grenades of criticism lobbed at him from his big brother and from Goliath. It is strange to think that people on both sides of the battlefield, Philistine and Israelite, were taking shots at David. This is to be expected from your enemy, but can be shocking and painful when it comes from someone on your side of the battle lines, and even from within your own family. David doesn't get a lot of affirmation along the way and there will be times you won't either. When you get real serious about trusting God and facing your Goliath, there's a chance some people will feel threatened by your boldness. They might even want to hold you back, especially if they are unwilling to face their own Goliath.

Read I Samuel 17:28 – 32, 41 – 44

5. Both Eliab and Goliath attacked David with harsh words of criticism. What is the nature of each of their attacks?

Describe an instance when you were assaulted verbally and how you responded.

6. When you face criticism and opposition, how do you tend to respond?

What steps might you take to respond with greater boldness the next time you are criticized?

Boldness While Being Pressed to Conform

David grew bolder as he faced and resisted the pressure to conform. This is something all of us will deal with in our daily lives. King Saul invited David to wear his armor and go into battle the way Saul would have. It would have been easy for David to say, "You know, Saul knows more than me when it comes to war. He has been at this longer. I'll do it his way." But David knew something very important. He knew *himself*, he knew his *enemy*, and he knew *God*. David knew that when he went to face Goliath, he would stand alone. Saul was not going to be there, his brothers would not be at his side, and even his dad could not help him. So, he had to go as one person and one person only ... David.

Read I Samuel 17:38–40

7. Saul's effort to conform David into a mini-Saul was not mean-spirited. He was trying to be helpful. How does David respond to Saul's suggestions and how can this help you know how to respond to people who want you to conform to their idea of who you should be?

8. Describe a time when you resisted the pressure to conform. How did that go?

*How did your effort to be yourself in this situation help grow bold-
ness in your heart?*

9. Name a situation you are currently facing in which someone
    is trying to get you to conform.

*What action or step do you need to take as you resist this tempta-
tion and boldly seek to be who God has made you?*

Boldness in the Great Crisis Moments of Life

The summary of the David and Goliath story is found in 1 Samuel
17:45 where David says, "You come against me with sword and spear
and javelin, but I come against you in the name of the LORD Almighty, the
God of the armies of Israel, whom you have defied." When the biggest
battle of all erupted right in front of David, he was ready because he had
seen God's faithfulness over and over again.

Goliath never counted on what he faced that day. Goliath had been
through a lot of battles. He had been a fighting man since his youth.
Imagine Goliath's shock! Here's a skinny kid with no armor, no military
experience, no sword, no javelin, no spear, no nothing! David came with
weapons Goliath had never seen in battle. He came only with the God of
Israel at his side, a bold heart beating in his chest, and a sling and stones.
David hurled a single rock, and it was all over. Goliath never expected
things to end this way.

Read I Samuel 17:45 – 50

10. You might have grown up hearing the David and Goliath story, but in this session you have looked at it in depth and with some fresh perspective. What is one new lesson that came out of this study and how will this impact your life?

11. The prayers and support of others help us face the Goliaths in our lives. How can your small group members stand at your side, cheer you on, and support you as you face your Goliath?

Celebrating and Being Celebrated

All through the Bible people told stories of God's victories, wonders, miracles, and mighty deliverance. Take a few moments to share stories of "Goliath Moments" your group members have faced. When was a time that you and God stood side-by-side and watched a Goliath fall?

Loving and Being Loved

Eliab and David's other brothers suffered from sickness in their spirit that might be called the "Goliath Syndrome." Every day that Goliath came out and issued his challenge, they became a little more infected. After forty days, it was chronic! It is the same kind of sickness that grips our souls when we respond in fear rather than boldness when our "Goliath Moments" come along.

In today's session we saw how Eliab, the oldest son of Jesse, harshly criticized David when David offered to fight Goliath. At that moment it seemed all brotherly love went out the window. Eliab didn't mind being around his other brothers because they were all afraid of Goliath! When David came along and expressed God-anointed boldness, Eliab felt like a coward. He saw somebody who was really bold and the contrast was painful.

In the face of David's defiant courage, Eliab felt ashamed. Fear made him unable to love David or to affirm his brother's gifts. Fear does that. It destroys love. We can feel okay when we're around other people who are also living in fear, but when we're with somebody who dares to challenge Goliath, we see our own cowardice by comparison and it doesn't feel good. Then, without even thinking, we can treat others with harshness rather than love.

Take time in the coming week to quietly reflect on your life. Do you have a case of the "Goliath Syndrome"? Is there anyone in your life who is living with boldness in an area where you tend to run and hide? Have you become resentful or critical of them? If so, confess that resentfulness to God. Then, spend some time praying for the person you have grown to resent. Ask for the Holy Spirit to fill your heart with love for this person and give you a new boldness in your heart and life. You may even want to send a note affirming them and letting them know you are praying for them.

Serving and Being Served

As a small group identify a person who you know is facing a "Goliath Moment" in their life. Make a commitment, as a group, to serve this person or family in the following ways:

- Pray together for God's power and blessing on their life. Pray also for them to have great boldness as they stand against their Goliath.
- Take time before you close for each person to write a note of encouragement to this person.
- Identify one way your group can take action that will fortify and support this person in their battle.

Hope for a Discouraged Heart

I SAMUEL 18–24, 30

Who you are, the test of your character, is not based on how you respond when things go well. It's how you respond when you're in the valley of discouragement.

David faced levels of discouragement that would have devastated most people. At the high point in David's life, the bottom fell out. As we reflect on his story, we find hope and encouragement for when our hearts become discouraged or we face deep loss.

David had been anointed by the prophet Samuel and was promised the throne of his nation. He was employed by Saul, the king, and had a place of influence and power. He defeated Goliath and was a national hero. The women of Israel were writing songs about him. Everything he touched turned to gold. What could go wrong? David was riding a wave of success and popularity that few in history could rival.

Then a funny thing happened. One by one, all of those wonderful things were stripped away.

David lost his job. He had been promoted from shepherd to court musician. He had also been exalted from an ordinary laborer to the most successful officer in the army of Israel. Then, with little warning, King Saul became pathologically jealous and tried to kill David. David escaped and ran for his life. And, in the snap of a finger, he lost his job, income, and occupational security. He went from being part of Israel's elite inner-circle to being a fugitive.

David lost his wife. He had married Saul's daughter, Michal. But when Saul turned against David, he also took away Michal and made her marry another man.

David fled to Ramah, home of the prophet Samuel, his friend and mentor. But Saul sent soldiers to Ramah and David had to flee. Samuel was an old man and could not go with him. And, a short time later, Samuel died. Now David had lost his closest spiritual brother and encourager.

Then David went to his best friend, Jonathan, the one person in the world David knew he could trust with anything. But Jonathan was also the son of Saul, and he could not raise a sword against his own father. So David had to run for his life once again and leave his closest friend behind.

David was on the "most wanted" list on the wall of every post office in Israel, so he ran and ran and ran until he got to Gath in the territory of the Philistines—Israel's mortal enemy. When King Achish of Gath heard David was in their territory, David was so fearful for his life that he pretended to be insane, scratching walls and letting saliva run down his face and beard.

Finally, David ended up living in caves in the wilderness, a hunted man. He had lost his job, family, spiritual mentor, closest friend, wealth, power, beauty, security, dignity, and country. Can you imagine a more discouraging scenario? And he lived this way for the next ten years! David was in a cave, literally. But he was also in the cave of discouragement, a place where all of us will spend time in the course of our lives.

Making the Connection

1. Describe a time you experienced sudden and unexpected loss and the discouragement you felt as a result.

2. How can times of deep loss and discouragement impact a person's faith and relationship with God?

Knowing and Being Known

Read I Samuel 20:30 – 42; 21:10 – 15; 22:1 – 2

Life in a Cave

The cave is where you end up when all of your props and crutches and scaffolding get stripped away. Maybe it's a lost job, financial pressures, dreams of a family life that have been shattered, loss of a spouse, brokenness in a good friendship, pain in a relationship with a parent, health problems, consequences of a bad decision, or something else. But, for whatever reason, you feel like everything is crashing down around you. The truth is, sooner or later everybody spends some time in the cave.

What's hardest about being in the cave is you sometimes wonder, *Has God lost track of me? Has he forgotten his promises? Does he still hear me? Will I die here or is there a way out of this cave?*

What we need to learn is this: God does some of his best work in caves. The cave is where he molds and shapes human lives like no other place. When all the props and crutches get stripped away, we learn that God really is enough. Sometimes, of all the places in this world, it's not the palace but the cave where God meets us and transforms us. This was true for David and it can be true in your life as well.

3. David was anointed by Samuel and promised the throne of Israel, only later to find himself a fugitive, living in caves a long way from the palace and with no crown on his head. In light of the passages you just read, describe the contrast between what David had anticipated and what he was living.

4. Respond to this statement: God does some of his best work in caves.

How have you experienced this to be true in your life?

How to Encourage Yourself in the Lord ...
Be Honest with God!

In one of David's darkest moments he made one of the greatest statements in the entire Bible. The King James Version translates it like this: "But David encouraged himself in the LORD" (1 Samuel 30:6). It's a wonderful thing to be encouraged by other people, but when you're in a cave and there's nobody to turn to, you can still be encouraged ... by God.

If you want to be encouraged in the Lord, the first thing you must do is discuss your discouragement openly with God. You've got to name it. This will take some time and effort. The superscription above Psalm 142 says, "A *maskil* of David. When he was in the cave. A prayer." This is a psalm written during a cave time, recorded for cave dwellers of all generations.

Read Psalm 142

NOTE: *Have a member of your group read this psalm aloud with the kind of passion a cave dweller might have prayed it.*

5. If you had been there and heard David lift up this passionate and honest prayer, what would you have learned about *one* of the following?

    *   David's understanding of prayer

    *   David's relationship with God

    *   The cave David was living in

6. Take a moment and write a brief "cave psalm" of your own. Use the space provided to write an honest, heartfelt description of what you are facing and how you are feeling.

    My Cave Psalm . . .

How to Encourage Yourself in the Lord ... Take Positive Action

Sometimes people get stuck in chronic discouragement because they don't devote the time or energy needed to discover its cause. They're just waiting for some outside force to change the situation when God is calling *them* to take action. One common example is discouragement in marriages. Neil Warren, a Christian psychologist, says that what kills marriages more than anything else is a lack of hope. When hope dies, the motivation to change is buried with it. Then the marriage partners quit trying. His recommendation is brilliantly simple: "Take one area in your marriage where you get discouraged and try to make a 10 percent improvement in a twelve-month period. If you do this, there will be a huge difference because hope is reborn." This simple commitment to make a small adjustment and take intentional action works in so many areas of life. Just give it a try.

Read 1 Samuel 30:1 – 20

7. What were some of the positive actions David took when he faced this discouraging situation?

    How might things have been different had David not taken this action?

8. When you think of a cave you are in right now, what is a specific, positive action you could take to move back outside?

33

How to Encourage Yourself in the Lord ...
Resist the Shortcut Temptation

There is a very important connection between temptation and being in a cave. When you're in the cave, when you're in a dark era of life, you will be uniquely vulnerable to any temptation that promises to get you out of the cave or to give you a few moments of relief. When such temptations come, you have to make a decision: Will you submit to God's will or take the easy way out?

Read I Samuel 24:1 – 7

9. What are some of the rationalizations and justifications that could have gone through David's mind when he faced the temptation to kill Saul and walk out of the cave that day?

10. Describe a time when you were in a cave and faced a tempting shortcut that would have gotten you out or offered temporary relief.

How to Encourage Yourself in the Lord ...
Discover Your Ultimate Refuge

Sometimes you will find yourself in a cave that just seems to hold you captive despite your efforts. You name it for what it is, you take action, you resist temptations, you do all the right stuff ... but you are still in the cave. Now what? At that moment all you can do is hang onto God and discover that he is your ultimate refuge. David uses the word *refuge* over and over again in the Psalms. Finding ultimate refuge in God means getting yourself so immersed in God's presence, so convinced of his goodness, and so devoted to his lordship that you find even the cave is a safe place because God is there with you.

Read Psalm 31:1 – 5

11. How have you experienced God's refuge during a time of pain, loss, or struggle?

Celebrating and Being Celebrated

Some of your group members just gave testimony of how they have experienced God as their source of refuge. Take time to pray as a group and thank God for being their refuge, shelter, and mighty tower in times of need. Use Psalm 31:1 – 5 to direct and inspire your prayers.

> In you, O LORD, I have taken refuge;
>> let me never be put to shame;
>> deliver me in your righteousness.
> Turn your ear to me,
>> come quickly to my rescue;
> be my rock of refuge,
>> a strong fortress to save me.
> Since you are my rock and my fortress,
>> for the sake of your name lead and guide me.
> Free me from the trap that is set for me,
>> for you are my refuge.
> Into your hands I commit my spirit;
>> redeem me, O LORD, the God of truth.

Loving and Being Loved

God understands all about caves because he has been there. Jesus suffered *like* us and he suffered *for* us. Our Savior had everything stripped away from him. He lost his position as a teacher; he lost his safety, and his friends ran away from him. Along the way Jesus lost the adoration of a cheering crowd, had his life threatened by his enemies, and finally went to a cross and died.

Do you remember where Jesus' body was buried after he had been abused and crucified? In a cave! They thought he was finished. They thought it was over. But what they didn't know, what the Evil One always forgets, is that God does some of his best work in caves. Caves are where God resurrects dead stuff.

They thought the cave could hold him. They thought death was final. But Jesus stayed in the cave for only three days. Then he rose again and walked out of the cave. When Jesus rose and left the cave, he declared to heaven and earth that caves won't win the day. Death is not final. His love won the ultimate battle.

There is no greater love than the love of God revealed in Jesus as he died on the cross, as he allowed them to put him in a cave, and as he rose in power and glory. His empty cave assures all those who love him that caves are never permanent. Accept this great love, thank Jesus for it, and hold his hand tightly every time you find yourself in a cave.

Serving and Being Served

In this session your group discussed how taking positive action is one of the ways we can encourage ourselves in the Lord. It is also a way to begin moving out of some of the cave experiences we face. Sometimes corporate action is more powerful than the efforts of one person. If one of your group members shared a cave experience that could be eliminated by the support of others, consider working together as a group to serve this person. Some possible examples might be:

Cave: A single mother is struggling with feeling she never gets time for herself.

Group Action: Offer to help with child care a couple times a month so she can get some personal time.

Cave: A man in the group is struggling with the temptation of consuming negative images in movies and on the Internet.

Group Action: A couple of the men in the group commit to keep him accountable and check up on how he is doing once a week for the coming month.

Cave: A couple is in a time of relational tension and struggle.

Group Action: An older couple offers to mentor them and once a month spend time talking with them about ways to grow a healthy marriage.

Cave ...
Action ...

A Contrite Heart

2 SAMUEL 11–12

Sin is the most destructive force the human race has ever encountered. It has caused more devastation than nuclear bombs and claimed more lives than any disease. And, like it or not, we all struggle with sin.

It might come in the form of deeply cutting words that depart from your mouth ... angry words, bitter words, sharp sarcasm that wounds the heart or veiled gossip that destroys the reputation of others. Maybe a kind of arrogant, judgmental spirit lives in your heart and pops up through the course of your week. Perhaps your life is caught up in a web of deception; you've told so many untruths that you hardly know right from wrong anymore. It could be coldness in your heart toward God or apathy about spiritual things that should matter to you. Sin comes in countless shapes and forms, but it comes knocking on each of our doors, more often than we want to admit.

Sin played as big a part in David's life as it does in our own. Ironically, although David was called a man after God's own heart, the story of his affair with Bathsheba and the downward spiral that followed is one of the most well known. It is a story about the sinister power of sin and God's desire to free us from its clutches. And it occurs in a season of David's life when he is no longer dwelling in caves or running from a mad king. Now he is the king, he has the throne, he wears the crown, and some of the passion of his younger years has waned.

The question is: How could it happen? How could a man who loved, served, and worshiped God with such passion end up in this deep pit of sin? In the story of David and Bathsheba we are forced to face a truth that we don't like to talk about. Every human being—everyone—is fallen, and we will all wrestle with sin until the day we die.

Followers of Christ sometimes divide sin into two categories. We never talk about it like this, but we sometimes view certain sins as acceptable and others as scandalous. God doesn't view things this way. He just sees sin. He sees fallen people who need his grace and redemption.

Making the Connection

1. What are some of the sins we might unconsciously label as "acceptable"?

   What sins are most commonly seen as scandalous (the really bad sins)?

   Though not intentional, why do you think so many people make these kinds of distinctions?

2. Although none of us likes to think about the reality, power, and consequences of sin, why is it important that we take time to look closely at sin and acknowledge its presence and power in our lives?

Read 2 Samuel 11

3. Sin gives birth to more sin. Identify the different sins committed by David in this story and how specific sinful attitudes, choices, and actions led to more sin.

4. What were some of the moments along the way that David could have stopped and cut off this chain reaction of sinful behavior?

5. What are some of the seasons and experiences in life that can create an atmosphere for a drifting heart to grow?

Crossroads #1: The Spiritual Drift Factor

The first crossroads David faced is found in 2 Samuel 11:1, where it says that it was spring and the whole Israelite army had gone off to war. But David remained in Jerusalem. This is a significant line: the time that "kings go off to war." Just like the Cubs go to Arizona for spring training, the swallows return to Capistrano, and taxes are due, every spring battles would be fought in the ancient world. But this year was different. David thought to himself, *I don't want to go. I don't have to go. Let the officers and soldiers go without me.* Back in 1 Samuel 8:20 the Israelites declared that they wanted a king who would go before them and lead them into battle. David had always done that ... but not this year. David was beginning to drift!

Some scholars think that the writer is cueing us into something important. We can kind of read between the lines. It was generally believed that David was about fifty years old at this time—not an old man, but no longer the golden boy either. Women didn't look at him the same way they used to. He started using Rogaine. He told himself he was going to work out a little more, get a jogging track installed around the palace. He might have secretly sprinkled Metamucil into his royal diet.

As David aged, he perhaps started to wonder if God really had his best interest at heart. Maybe he began to think, as so many of us do, *I'm going to have to look out for myself. If I don't take care of my needs and wants, who will?* What David should have done at this critical crossroads was to spend time alone with God and anchor his heart back to the One who had provided, protected, and delivered him so many times in the past. Instead, he let his heart drift toward the jagged rocks of sin.

6. When you feel your heart begin to drift toward sin, what specific actions do you take to stop the drift?

Crossroads #2: Spiritual Warning Lights

First, David's heart began to drift. But he did not seem to notice, or at least did nothing to stop it. Instead, he took another step toward sin. When he noticed a beautiful woman bathing, he sent someone to gather information about her. The response came quickly, "Isn't this Bathsheba, the daughter of Eliam and the wife of Uriah the Hittite?" It was subtle, but the second crossroads—now that David faced a specific temptation—was the little phrase "the wife of Uriah the Hittite." Through the messenger, God was flashing a spiritual warning light for David: "This is somebody's wife. This is somebody's daughter. Be careful!"

At our own crossroads, we may hear the inner voice of the Spirit, a message of conscience, or words from a friend that warn us: trouble ahead. It's interesting to watch how people respond to a yellow light at an intersection. Some hit the brakes and slow down. Some hit the accelerator and blast through. When God flashes a spiritual warning light, it is always good to hit the brakes.

7. Pick one of the following sins and list a few possible warning lights God might flash to get a person's attention and slow them down.

    • Speaking harsh and hurtful words toward family members.
    • Living with a selfish, greedy spirit and lifestyle.
    • Indulging in pornography or "romance novels" that paint inappropriate pictures in our hearts and minds.
    • Becoming consumed with work, accomplishments, and the praise of people while neglecting a growing relationship with God.
    • Some other area of sin: _____

    _____

Possible Warning Lights:
    1.

    2.

    3.

Crossroads #3: How We Respond After We Have Sinned

Sin always sets in motion spiritually destructive forces that cannot be controlled. It may be external forces like pregnancy, in David's case. It could be internal forces: the loss of integrity, the loss of character, or the loss of innocence.

Once David had crossed the line by committing adultery with Bathsheba, he faced the next crossroads. How would he respond now that the results of his sin had spun out of his control? We all come to this crossroads. How do you respond after you've sinned and you realize that what you have done is wrong? How do you react when the consequences start to unfold? The options are fairly simple: we can fall on our knees, confess our sins, and repent ... or we can try to cover up our sin and keep running from God.

Review 2 Samuel 11:5 – 27

8. When David heard that Bathsheba was pregnant, he opted to "cover up" rather than confess and repent. What were some of the things David did to hide his sin?

What were some of the costs of David's cover-up scheme?

9. Keeping with the same sin you chose for question 7 on page 42, write down some of the possible consequences should a person decide to justify, rationalize, and cover up.

Possible Consequences:

1.

2.

3.

Crossroads #4: Facing Consequences and God's Judgment

David had blasted through every crossroads without touching the brakes. His heart had been drifting for some time; he did not notice. Warning lights were flashing; he accelerated. The consequences of his sin were announced to him; he covered up. What else could God do to get his attention? David had exhausted all options but one: God's judgment. Not a judgment to destroy, but a severe love designed to wake up David and bring him home. Like a loving parent with a spoiled, rebellious child, God took a firm and loving step: he disciplined his son, David.

Read 2 Samuel 12:1 – 13

10. Sometimes when we read the Bible we can miss the emotion of the unfolding drama. This passage pulsates with raw emotion, some on the surface and some just under the surface. Discuss the emotion that must have existed in *one* of the primary players in this scene:
    • David

    • Nathan

    • God

11. Tell about a time when God brought loving discipline into your life.

How did God's discipline bring transformation in this area?

Celebrating and Being Celebrated

Read Psalm 51

The superscription above Psalm 51 reads: "For the director of music. A psalm of David. When the prophet Nathan came to him after David had committed adultery with Bathsheba."

This psalm poured out of David's heart after the darkest season in his life. It is about confession of past sin, but also a declaration of hope for the future. Identify hope-filled statements and let these guide your group in a time of prayer celebrating the hope that exists for all who confess their sins, repent, and receive God's grace.

Loving and Being Loved

David thought that the great danger of his life was that somebody might find out about his sin. Of course, that wasn't his greatest danger. His greatest danger was that no one would find out, and his soul would be utterly destroyed. That's always the way it is with sin. In the same way, our great danger is that nobody will find out, and we'll end up living in darkness.

In the book of James we read these words:

> Therefore confess your sins to each other and pray for each other so that you may be healed. The prayer of a righteous man is powerful and effective. (James 5:16)

If you have an area of sin in your life that you have kept hidden for weeks, months, or years, consider this amazing act: Find a person you trust, who will exercise confidentiality, and confess your sin to them. Ask for their prayers, encouragement, and accountability as you seek to repent of this sin.

Serving and Being Served

Have you ever heard someone say, "I saw that coming"? Maybe a marriage breaks up, a business deal goes south, or someone faces a moral crash. Then, someone quietly and knowingly whispers, "I saw that coming." Maybe you have made this comment to others or even whispered it to yourself after sin brings down another victim.

Consider this radical and courageous act of service. Make yourself available to be a Nathan. Say to God, "If I see sin growing in a friend's life, rebellion capturing a family member's heart, or hints of disobedience showing up in the behavior of someone I love, I am available to speak the truth to them. I will be a Nathan. Even though I am aware of my own sin and weaknesses, I will seek to be a truth-speaker. If God calls me to say something, I will do it gently, I will do it humbly, I might even do it with trembling knees, but I will do it."

A Broken Heart

2 SAMUEL 13–18

Of all the kinds of heartbreak a human being can experience there's none sadder than relational heartbreak. Picture a couple standing before a judge in divorce court. Their minds go back to the day they stood before a minister and recited their vows to each other. They were filled with anticipation, hope, dreams, and so much love. They started well. Then, things slowly deteriorated. Like a sand castle along the beach as the tide came in, things seemed to melt away. They never dreamed it would end up so poorly. Quietly each one wonders, *How did it come to this?*

Picture best friends who went into business together. Joy and excitement defined the beginning of this new enterprise, with comments such as: "We can't believe we get to do this together. We get to be partners. We are going to share life's challenges and successes ... mostly the successes!" But somewhere along the line the wheels fall off. Their friendship splinters and begins to break under the financial and emotional pressures. They end up having to dissolve the business through third-party mediators. As the assets are divided, they struggle to speak to each other or make eye contact, both wondering, *How did it come to this?*

David wrote a beautiful psalm that begins, "How good and pleasant it is when God's people live together in unity!" (Psalm 133:1 TNIV). In the same way, David could have written, "How painful and unpleasant it is when God's people experience division and disunity."

David experienced both ends of the emotional spectrum in his relationships. He knew amazing moments of unity and he also saw close relationships implode. Perhaps the most tragic of all his relational breakdowns was with his son Absalom. It began with a son who loved and respected his father and a father who adored his son. It ended with David weeping over his son's death at the hand of David's own military commander.

If brothers and sisters are really going to dwell together in unity, one thing is for certain: It will take work. It often seems the natural entropy of life leads to relational disunity and broken hearts. We can see this everywhere we look. But, as we look at the journey of David and Absalom, we can learn to love in new ways that can transform how we relate to others and minimize the chance of relational heartbreak.

Making the Connection

1. Sadly, many relationships break down and lead to heartache. What are some things we can do to help any relationship grow strong and healthy?

Knowing and Being Known

A Biblical Horror Story

If the story you are about to read were made into a movie, it would get a firm R rating and deserve it. It is a painful account to digest, but the Bible never tries to cover up people's wrong actions nor sin's reality. The Bible tells all: the good, the bad, and the ugly—and this story is ugly. It is important to read because it reveals the beginning of David and Absalom's long journey to relational brokenness.

Amnon and Tamar were both David's children, but by different mothers. Tamar was Absalom's full sister. When David heard about what Amnon did to Tamar, "he was furious." The problem is, he did nothing about it. The Bible tells us that Tamar lived in her brother Absalom's house, a desolate woman. Two years passed after the assault on Tamar and there were still no repercussions for Amnon or vindication for Tamar. This was a recipe for relational and family devastation on many levels. As you read this story, remember: these are real people in a real family.

Read 2 Samuel 13:1 – 23

2. Choose *one* of the following options and write a brief but honest letter (imagining you are the person in the story) expressing how you feel about the state of your relationship two years after this incident has transpired:

   • From Absalom to David
   • From Absalom to Amnon
   • From Absalom to Tamar
   • From Tamar to Amnon
   • From Tamar to David

I am writing to tell you how I feel toward you today ...

   Have a few people read their letter to the group, explaining why they feel it reflects the emotions this person might have felt and the state of their relationship.

3. Write down the name of a person in your life with whom you are experiencing relational strain or brokenness:

_____

Take a moment for silent prayer so that each person in your group can ask God to help bring healing to this relationship.

Love Confronts

Tamar was the victim of Amnon's heartless attack, but many relationships were damaged along the way. One was that of Absalom (Tamar's brother) and his father David. Absalom was so upset that his father did nothing about Amnon's attack that he decided to take things into his own hands. David refused to confront Amnon and deal with his sinful actions, and things got progressively worse for the whole family.

When we love someone, we are willing to confront them when they have wronged us or someone else. We don't stand by passively and hope the problem disappears, because it never does. It could be a conflict with someone at work and you are not dwelling together in unity. Maybe there is relational strain with a family member, but you don't want to make waves. It could even be with a member of your church or small group. As we look at David's story, we discover that silence, in these situations, is not the way of love. There are times in life when we need to make a decision to confront, because we love the person and we long for a restoration of unity.

Read 2 Samuel 13:23 – 39

4. We have to be honest and admit that sometimes loving confrontation is not received as well as we might hope. Name some ways people might respond to us if we confront them about a sinful pattern or behavior in their life.

5. David's family faced greater turmoil and brokenness because he refused to confront. Tell about a time when you confronted someone in a loving way and the result was restoration and healing.

6. You are in a conversation with a friend who declares, "I would never confront someone who has wronged me. I don't like the tension it brings. I just pray and hope the problem will go away." What counsel would you give this person?

Love Listens

Sometimes love needs to listen. What Absalom needed most was a father who would listen and let him express his grief and frustration. But David was not there for him. Absalom tried to reach his dad through Joab: "Help me see my dad. I've got to talk to my dad." But Joab wouldn't help bridge the broken communication between father and son. Joab knew what David's response would be … he did not want to speak with Absalom. For two years Absalom lived in Jerusalem—allowed back in the city, but not allowed access to the palace or his father. It was a public, painful silent treatment.

Finally Absalom was so desperate that he openly set fire to Joab's fields. He wanted to be caught. In essence Absalom was saying, "I have to do something to get my dad's attention. I have to see my father. Let him condemn me if he wants to. If he tells me I've done something wrong, and he's going to kill me, let him kill me. Or if he's going to love me, let him love me. But anything is better than this. I can't do this anymore!" These two years of noncommunication fueled the fire for what would come next.

Read 2 Samuel 14:23–32

7. In desperation, Absalom set fire to Joab's field in hopes of getting his father's attention. Every day people "set fires" when they are facing the pain of a broken relationship and when they don't feel heard. What are some of the "fire-setting" things people do?

8. Name one person in your life for whom you need to make time to offer a loving and listening ear.

How can your group members support you in prayer as you seek to strengthen this relationship by listening more attentively?

Read 2 Samuel 15:1–15; 18:1–17; 18:32–33

Love Speaks

When Absalom died, David had a moment of clarity. The problem is that these moments often come too late. After he learned of his son's death, he began to say the things he should have been saying all along. This can happen to any of us if we are not careful. We should ask ourselves, on a regular basis, "Is there something I need to say?" Maybe it's, "I'm sorry, please forgive me." Maybe it's, "I love you." Maybe it's, "I forgive you." Or maybe it's, "Let's try again."

There might be weeks, months, or years of distance and stubborn pride that keep you from speaking words of love. But we can learn from David and not repeat what he did. We do not have to consign ourselves to a lifetime of regret. If there is a word that needs to be said in your relational world, it is time to speak.

9. Tell about a time you spoke loving and grace-filled words into a broken relationship and the end result was healing and restoration.

10. Who is someone that needs to hear loving words from you? If they were sitting with you right now, what would you tell them?

How can your group members keep you accountable to share these words with this person?

Celebrating and Being Celebrated

One of the best ways to celebrate another person is to speak words of blessing. In this session you identified a person who needs to hear loving words from you. Commit to contact this person and express these words. This can be face-to-face, by phone, via email or handwritten note. If you have words that have gone unspoken for too long, don't wait. Let them flow and pray that they will lead to a deeper, richer, more loving relationship.

Loving and Being Loved

Confrontation rarely feels like a loving action … at least not at the time. Talk as a group about becoming a community of people who will lovingly confront each other and receive confrontation. This is not entry-level, 101 community. This is advanced stuff, for those who truly want to grow in Christian maturity.

Consider using the following question in your group gatherings as a way to create a place of loving confrontation:

What attitude or action do you see growing in me that might dishonor God or others? How can I adjust this attitude or action to live a more Christ-honoring life?

Serving and Being Served

There are people in every church who seem to face an unusually high level of relational brokenness. They need people around them who will express love, care, and offer a listening ear. Take time as a group to identify someone who could use some encouragement, a word of blessing, or a helpful hand. Identify how your group can come alongside this person (or family) and be God's agent of heart-healing love.

A Generous Heart

I SAMUEL 30; 2 SAMUEL 24

I think one of the most amazing moments in the development of a human being is when a child utters their first word. Parents wait for that moment with bated breath. Sometimes they try very hard to accelerate it by working with their child on speech development (and sometimes they regret that later).

Some mothers and fathers spend hours coaching their child to make sure their first word is *mama* or *dada*, depending on the gender of the parent. That always seemed kind of silly to me, so I've never made a big deal out of the fact that all three of our kids said "dada" before they said "mama."

Soon after they learn *dada* and *mama*, children learn their next important word: *no*! Psychologists tell us it's a very significant word. It helps the child individuate and set boundaries and assert his own sense of identity and autonomy. Psychologists say it's a good stage, this "no" stage, although most psychologists who say this have never had a small child of their own.

Also, right around this time in their language development, kids pick up another word. They use it a lot when someone else wants to play with one of their toys, or tries to wear their clothes, or taste their food, or touch their things. And the word, of course, is *mine*. "My toys, my stuff, my room, my food, mine!"

Some people go to their grave and it's still their favorite word. They might not say it out loud much, but it marks them. It's on their wallet; it's on their checkbook; it's on their house; it's on their car; it's on their time; it's on their life — "mine!"

Ultimately, this is the truth about human beings. The day will come when each of us will say one of two words to God from the core of our being. Either we will say, "*Yours*, God. Everything I have; everything I am; everything I own; it's all yours." Or we will say to him, "*Mine*. I give you nothing. I submit nothing."

And God will respond with one of two words: *heaven* or *hell*. By the first he means, "I receive you and your life as a gift." By the latter he means, "I'll allow you to be separate from me for all eternity."

Making the Connection

1. How does our culture create and encourage a "mine" attitude above a "yours" attitude?

2. How do a self-centered attitude and selfish lifestyle conflict with God's plan for those who seek to follow Jesus?

In what ways did Jesus model a sacrificial, yours-oriented life?

A Generous Heart ... Focuses on the Needs of Others

There were areas of life where David messed up royally. But one thing David got right was the call to live a generous life. David loved to give and share with others. He knew that a generous heart focuses on the needs of other people more than on personal discontent. This is hard to do when we live in a culture that tutors us in selfishness every day.

James Dusenberry, a post–World War II Harvard economist, wrote a classic piece about what drives the financial behavior of Americans. In it he coined the phrase, "Keeping up with the Joneses." This idea captures the pathology of consumption that drives us to work hard at jobs we don't like, to make money we don't need, to buy things we can't use, to impress people we don't even know. It is time that we just declare the Joneses the winner. We need to make a decision to stop comparing ourselves to what other people have. When we let go of this idol and stop playing the consumption game, we can discover the joy of caring about the needs of others rather than always thinking about ourselves.

Read I Samuel 30:9 – 26

3. How does David model and teach a generous lifestyle that focuses on the needs of others?

4. How might our lifestyles and priorities change if we made a daily effort to think about the needs of others?

5. What are some of the monetary needs experienced by people in your community?

What could you do as a small group to meet one of these needs in the coming weeks?

A Generous Heart ... Looks for Opportunities to Give

People with a generous heart are proactive or intentional about finding ways to give. They don't just wait until an opportunity presents itself; they look for chances to be generous. Some people even make a decision to consume less so they can give more. This might seem countercultural and even un-American, but it reflects the very heart of God.

This kind of lifestyle is hard to live out in a culture that dangles all sorts of "stuff" in front of us and invites us to consume. In an advertisement for a beautiful sofa the text read, "That's not tribal drums you're hearing. It's your heart." Another magazine displayed a beautiful car and the caption simply said, "You can't buy happiness, but now you can lease it." Marketing experts spend billions of dollars to convince us that we need more and more.

God wants us to learn an amazing spiritual dynamic. When you give, good things start to happen. They happen to the one who receives the gift, in the heart of the one who gives, and even to people who watch generosity unfold in a selfish world. That's why Jesus says, "Give, and it will be given back to you." When generosity wins, the darkness gets rolled back a bit, and a little crack forms in the kingdom of the Evil One. It's a divine act, a small miracle each time somebody gives.

Read 2 Samuel 24:18 – 25

6. How do you see David's heart of generosity toward Araunah and toward God?

7. Think of a person you know who is an example of generosity ... someone who just has a way of noticing needs and responding with gracious freedom. What is it about their life that inspires you?

8. How might limiting our spending and growing in contentment create opportunities for us to be more generous?

What is one way you could adjust your lifestyle to free up resources to share with others?

A Generous Heart ... Finds Joy in Giving

People with generous hearts find themselves overflowing with gladness as they give. They actually enjoy it! They know all they "have" is on loan from God—it is not theirs; they are not anxious or worried about the stuff of this world, because it really belongs to God. When this reality sets deep into our souls, we learn to have fun sharing God's stuff.

The apostle Paul wrote:

> Each of you should give what you have decided in your heart to give, not reluctantly or under compulsion, for God loves a cheerful giver. And God is able to bless you abundantly, so that in all things at all times, having all that you need, you will abound in every good work. (2 Corinthians 9:7–8 TNIV)

The paradox is that we're afraid to give generously because we think that having more stuff is the secret to happiness. In reality, we find greater joy when we learn to be generous. You will never meet a really, really happy, joyful greedy person.

Read 1 Chronicles 29:1–18

9. What are some of the signs that David and the people were actually finding joy in the process of giving toward God's work?

How do you see joy-filled giving becoming contagious among God's people as they gathered offerings for the temple?

10. How have you experienced deep and Spirit-given joy as you have grown in your commitment to give generously?

11. What is one step you can take to grow a little more generous in the coming year?

How can your group members encourage you in this growth and support you as you take this joy-filled step of faith?

Celebrating and Being Celebrated

Read 1 Chronicles 29:10 – 13

NOTE: *Read this prayer of David aloud as a group.*

David praised the LORD in the presence of the whole assembly, saying,
"Praise be to you, O LORD,
   God of our father Israel,
   from everlasting to everlasting.
Yours, O LORD, is the greatness and the power
   and the glory and the majesty and the splendor,
   for everything in heaven and earth is yours.

Yours, O Lord, is the kingdom;
    you are exalted as head over all.
Wealth and honor come from you;
    you are the ruler of all things.
In your hands are strength and power
    to exalt and give strength to all.
Now, our God, we give you thanks,
    and praise your glorious name.

Use this prayer as a springboard to lift up prayers of praise and celebration for God's generous goodness toward you.

Loving and Being Loved

Generous hearts increasingly seek opportunities to give. The truth is, they are all around you if you slow down and look. Maybe you know a child who could really use a secret scholarship to a Christian summer camp. Perhaps you know of a family who is really struggling and a grocery store or restaurant gift certificate would make a huge difference. Maybe you could sponsor a child through a mission organization, or volunteer time and/or resources to a local relief agency or city mission. Whatever the opportunity, make a choice to express God's love to those in need.

Serving and Being Served

If you want to be in a position and posture to give generously and to serve others with freedom and joy, view everything as God's and not yours. When you walk into your home, survey your possessions and say with great passion, "It's not my stuff." When you pull out your wallet and look at the credit cards and money, don't say to yourself, "There's not enough in there," as some of us do. Say with great passion, "It's not my stuff!"

If you want to take it a step further, make little labels that say "God's stuff" and put them in your car, closet, refrigerator—anywhere that might remind you to keep your perspective right. While you're at it, just slap one of those "God's stuff" labels on your forehead, because once you recognize that all you have belongs to God, you will realize that you belong to him too.

Session One –
What Matters Most to God? The Heart!
1 SAMUEL 16:1–13

Questions 1–2

When Israel first entered the Promised Land, God was the leader of the nation and used judges and prophets to give direction to the people. But the people still wanted a king, so God had Samuel anoint Saul as its first king. Saul was an impressive man, head and shoulders above the rest. But over time, he became increasingly corrupt, violent, and evil. In 1 Samuel 13:14 God said he would appoint a man after his own heart to sit on the throne.

At the point our story begins in 1 Samuel 16, Samuel is an old man. God calls him to go to Bethlehem and anoint a new king ... one of Jesse's sons. And Samuel says, "But God, we've already got a king, and it's not good for my health to appoint a new king when there's still an old one on the throne." And God said, "Trust me."

Samuel invites the elders and Jesse's family to a gathering. You might imagine that his arrival would create quite a stir in this obscure little village. Jesse is so proud he can hardly stand it. You've got to picture this scene for a moment. Jesse introduces his first son, his heir. Remember, birth order is everything back in those days.

Jesse has always known that Eliab was destined for greatness. He was class president, quarterback of the football team, and outstanding young CEO. The kid pulls up in a Jeep Grand Cherokee, and he has a commanding presence. He walks into a room and just dominates it. And Jesse says, "This is my son, Eliab." Eliab is Hebrew for "you the man." (Not really!)

Jesse says, "He's the man." The elders all nod their heads, "Yeah, he's the man." And Samuel looks at him and said, "Yeah, he's the man all right." But God says, "He's not the man."

Jesse has son number two, Abinadab, stand in front of the prophet, but he's not the man. And then sons numbers three, four, five, six, and seven ... none of them are "the man" either. So Samuel says to Jesse, "Are these the only sons you have?" That seems like a dumb question, doesn't it? Don't you think Jesse would be aware of how many sons he has? But Jesse says, almost as an afterthought, "There's still the youngest, but he's out with the sheep. He's not the man."

Samuel says, "Go send for him. We'll wait." So they just stand there, seven sons, all like the first runner-up in the Miss Universe pageant trying to look like things are okay when in truth they're hoping that the real winner gets disqualified so they can take over.

Finally David comes pulling up in a beat-up, used Yugo. God looks at David and says, "That's the one. That's him. He's the man!" Do you see the theme here? It is the classic reversal of birth order. Eliab is the natural for the job, but David, the youngest, is God's chosen.

This does not mean gifts or talents don't matter to God. Sometimes Christians talk as if things like gifts or strengths are bad things. They act as if God prefers people who have no talent at all. The problem is this denies the doctrine of creation which says that God made all things, including talents and gifts and strengths. God gave them out, and God fully intends to redeem them; he wants them to shine gloriously.

What this account points out is *not* that gifts, talents, or strengths are bad things or things that God can't use. What it points out is that the human race inevitably tends to obsess over external appearance. We tend to think that charm, attractiveness, and ability are all that matter. What God says over and over is that in his kingdom everybody matters. In God's kingdom everybody has got something to offer; everybody's contribution matters, the last-born as well as the firstborn.

Questions 3–5

David was so passionate about God and expressed his praise with such wild abandon that he started jumping up and down ... he danced before God. His wife Michal tried to rein him in, embarrassed by his "excessive enthusiasm." But David let her, and everyone else, know that he was committed to celebrate God's goodness, with even greater reckless passion.

This characteristic shows up in David's life a number of times in 1–2 Samuel. For instance, 2 Samuel 23 recounts the time when David and his mighty men are pinned down by a band of Philistines. David has tremendous thirst and cries out for water from a well that he knows of near Jerusalem. In response, three of his top warriors risk their lives, break through enemy lines to reach the well, draw water, and return to their leader.

This is a moment of unbelievable drama. All the troops are gathered when they give David the water he so longed for. Though all are parched by thirst, there's only enough water for the king. So moved is David by their courage and their sacrifice that he takes the water and pours it out on the ground. In so doing it's as if he's saying, "I'll be with you in thirst and deprivation as well as in prosperity. I will not use the kingship to get my comfort at the expense of your pain. We're in this together, you and me, win or lose, live or die." It's like a scene out of a Mel Gibson movie. What passion!

Wouldn't it be wonderful to have a heart like that? None of us wants to go to our grave with a heart that was cold, calculating, protected, and always safe. We should all long to be moved to give God unfettered praise and worship with a sense of abandon and sacrifice.

Questions 6–8

I think that I can make a case that the years when David's heart was most vulnerable to sin were after he had reached the top, become king, and had everything he wanted. It was at this time of his life that he felt he no longer had to be alone with God. We need to take care that this does not happen to us. We need to make space to develop a reflective heart.

You can't develop roots fast. Roots don't work that way. When was the last time you described someone by saying, "That person is hurried, frenzied, and deep"? You can be hurried or you can be deep, but you can't be both. You'll have to choose. This doesn't mean you have to quit your job and become a shepherd. That's not God's plan. But it does mean you will have to arrange for and guard regular, unhurried times alone with him.

Think of how we would be different if we all followed David's example and made time to be shepherded by God. It would be a great exercise to read through David's psalms (see the Serving and Being Served section) while doing this study on his life. Martin Luther regularly used the psalms to direct his prayers. When Jesus was on the cross he quoted from Psalm 22. Some of the psalms will allow you to express confusion or complaint. Others will teach about how to make heartfelt confession and lead you to places of authentic repentance. Some will lift you to places of prayerful ecstasy and praise.

Questions 9–10

Another example of David's stubborn love was the way he cared for Jonathan, Saul's son. Jonathan could have easily seen David as a rival for the throne of Israel. You would expect them to have been at each other's throats. Instead, they had one of the greatest friendships in history. And, when they had to be separated, the Bible says they wept together. "They wept together, but David wept the most."

Many years later, when Saul and Jonathan had both been dead for a long time, David said, "Is there anyone left of the house of Saul to whom I can show kindness for Jonathan's sake?" The people brought him a son of Jonathan, a man named Mephibosheth, who was crippled in both feet. Mephibosheth bowed before David, expecting the worst, because he could have been seen as a rival claimant to the throne. David looked at this powerless person and said, "Don't be afraid. I just want to love you. I want to give you back all the land that belonged to your grandfather and I want you to eat at my table. I want you to be like my son." What a stubborn, tenacious love!

Session Two — A Bold Heart
I SAMUEL 17:1–50

Question 1

The story of David and Goliath is *not* a story about David's raw courage, his skill with the sling, or his willingness to take a risk. This is a story about God. Likewise, the story of your life is not a story about your courage, skill, or willingness to take a risk. It is, if you will let it be, a story about God and the power he wants to unleash in your life as you face daily battles.

Questions 3–4

Imagine you're David in a field watching sheep — they're not even yours; they're your dad's sheep — and a bear comes along. You have no gun. You have a big stick. That's what David would have had. What would you do? David could have run. The only one to see him would have been the sheep, and they would never talk.

Sheep were not going to fight the bear. Sheep were not known for their courage. Nobody would have known if David ran away except David ... and God. What is amazing is that this young boy stayed and fought! And, in his day-by-day faithfulness in a thankless job, courage and boldness were born in his heart.

David doesn't say, "I learned that *I* could defeat lions and bears." He doesn't say, "I learned my own sufficiency." He says, "I learned that God, who delivered me from lions and bears, can deliver me from anything."

You can hear "God is faithful" a thousand times, and a lot of people have. You can read "God is faithful" in a hundred books, and a lot of people have. But you will only come to believe it down in the marrow of your bones when you test it out in real life.

When facing the ordinary challenges of life, we — like David — have an opportunity to stand boldly or run away. It was in the ordinary moments when nobody was watching, in an unglamorous job as a shepherd, that David, day after day, built a very bold heart. If he had waited until he faced Goliath, he would have run with everybody else. But he didn't. He took on everyday challenges — lions and bears — and God was faithful. Then, when the time came, he was ready to face the big challenges with the same boldness he had exhibited hundreds of times before in the daily stuff of life. This is the lesson we need to take to the construction site, to the office, into a long day at home with kids, and everywhere else we go.

Questions 5–6

All of Eliab's criticisms of David are cheap shots, not honest critique or helpful observations but mean-spirited, unfair attacks.

David had been sent by his father; he didn't come on his own. He was just being obedient. The sheep were being cared for by somebody else. But Eliab gives him jab after jab.

David's response is amazing. He does not let his big brother's words discourage him. He knows there is nothing to Eliab's charges. He presses on. Later, when Goliath begins launching taunts, David again presses on. He even throws a few words back at the giant war machine.

Too often we let the words and insecurity of others keep us from boldly following God's plan for our lives. We can learn a great deal from David. At the same time, if we are mature we will listen to heartfelt, caring critique. We can learn from others. But if we make an honest assessment, as David did, and realize that the words being directed at us are false and intended to crush our spirits, we will refuse to listen!

We will all face some opposition and criticism when we try to do what's right and honorable before God. Sometimes it might even come from a brother or sister, a close friend, or someone else we know and respect. When this happens, we can give up and lose heart; we can get defensive and fight back; or we can say, "This is what I think God is calling me to do, as best as I can discern." When we have such resolve in our hearts, we can get on with accomplishing the task God has given us. Along the way, our boldness will grow.

Questions 7–9

Saul puts all of his best stuff—his championship armor—on David, and David can't even walk. One writer put it like this: "Saul is a 52 long, David is like a 36 short." So David has to do a very bold thing. Remember, Saul is the king and David is just a subject. Saul is an impressive man, head and shoulders above everybody else in Israel. David is a kid. Saul is a warrior. David is a shepherd boy who has never been in battle. Yet David tells Saul that he can't go into battle dressed like Saul. He must go as David ... as a shepherd.

Though we may have wonderful fellowship and community, when we go to face Goliath, in a very real sense we always stand alone. Just as Saul tried to turn David into a miniature version of himself, people will suggest that we face our battles the way they would. There is only one problem: it is not their battle; it is ours. At the end of the day, we must choose how we will go to battle. And, every time we face our Goliath as God has made us, we grow a little bolder.

Questions 10–11

David prepared for his "Goliath Moment" as he learned boldness in the ordinary experiences of daily life as a shepherd. His heart grew bolder as he pressed past criticism and opposition. Then, he grew even stronger as he learned to be himself and not bow to the pressure to conform to what others thought he should be. Now, he was ready to face a major challenge because the furnace of countless little choices had forged a heart that was ready for this moment.

Session Three – Hope for a Discouraged Heart
I SAMUEL 18–24, 30

Questions 1–2

We all face times when the bottom falls out. In these moments we can give up and let discouragement rule our hearts. Or, we can encourage ourselves in the Lord and accept his grace and strength. These seasons of life can crush us into dust or press us into diamonds. God's desire is to see us become something even more beautiful through these times.

Questions 5–6

Old Testament scholars tell us about the different kinds of psalms: thanksgiving psalms, wisdom psalms, enthronement psalms about the kings. But the number one category, the most frequent type of psalm, is the psalm of lament, which is just a fancy word for "complaint." Apparently, God is not put off by this at all; he invites his people to do this. And that's why David so often goes before the Lord, digs down to the very bottom of his pain and discouragement, and honestly expresses his heart.

Not many people have the courage to pray with this kind of authenticity. They stuff their discouragement down deep. They pretend everything is fine when they are struggling with life and God. They put on a stoic exterior, force a few smiles. But they avoid the pain that's inside of them. That doesn't solve anything. As a matter of fact, it usually leads to real problems.

Some people live with such a chronic sense of discouragement that they get used to it. They don't even notice that they are so full of pain that it leaks out of them, robbing them of life and joy—and draining the life out of other people. This is not God's will for anyone.

God is never a God of discouragement. When you have a discouraged spirit or thought, you can be sure it is not from God. This is not to say that God never brings hard things. God brings conviction of sin; he calls for repentance over fallenness; he brings challenges and even uses times of suffering to refine us and draw us close to him. But God is not about creating discouragement for his children. That is not what God is like.

Questions 7–8

When David returned to Ziklag and realized that the camp had been raided, he launched into action. Though there was mass discouragement and his own men were threatening his life, David did not fold. He took action.

David sought the counsel of the priest and sought the will of the Lord (1 Samuel 30:7); he gathered his men for a search-and-rescue mission (v. 9); he gathered information about those who had raided their camp (vv. 13–15); he led his men in battle (v. 17); he recovered all that had been taken (v. 18); and he brought it all home (v. 20). Talk about action, taking steps, doing something. And, when it was all said and done, David and his small band of people were out of the cave.

Questions 9–10

Notice what David's men said when Saul entered the cave where they were hiding and could easily have been murdered: "This is the day the LORD spoke of." In other words, "God promised you deliverance; now here it is. Saul is here. You can do away with him. You can kill him. That must be what God wants. God doesn't want you to be unhappy and miserable in this cave. He doesn't want you in the wilderness. Saul deserves judgment, heaven knows. This is a clear way out of the cave. It must be God's will."

This advice must have been so tempting for David. He must have thought, *I could get out of the cave right now*. He moved toward Saul but only cut off a corner of his robe, apparently to prove to Saul that he could have killed him. But David was conscience-stricken for even taking that action against the king. He knew taking Saul's life would have been wrong, a shortcut in God's plan. It certainly would have sent a message to everybody in Israel that the way to become the new king is to kill the old one. It would have ultimately destroyed David's soul.

Session Four — A Contrite Heart
2 SAMUEL 11 – 12

Question 3

In this episode of David's life he is guilty of lust, covetousness, deceit, adultery, and murder. Some people wonder if Bathsheba is partly at fault in this story. Why is she taking a bath outside where David could see her? Is she complicit in this sinful tragedy? There's nothing in the text that indicts her as being guilty.

Most likely, in the afternoon, the water in the rain barrels would be at its warmest. And at this time of year, the spring, the men would be off to war. That was where David was supposed to be. Her behavior is customary for the times ... there were no inside showers or bathing facilities.

Bathsheba is not seeking to enter any kind of inappropriate relationship, but David takes her anyway. There's no mention of how she feels, no record of what she says or what David says to her. Maybe she'll solve his boredom problem. Maybe she'll take away his feelings of loneliness. Bathsheba is treated as an object by David, something to be used. When sin gets ahold of you, that is how you treat people.

Questions 4 – 6

In this session we will look at four crossroads, four defining moments in this episode of David's life. Sadly, David just blew right past three of them. Every time he went past one and took the wrong road, things got worse.

Eugene Peterson notes that a key word that carries through the whole story is the little verb *send* or *sent*. It's used a number of times, mostly of David and the way he plays God in people's lives to get what he wants. He sends here and he sends there ... all to fulfill his sinful whims. David sends for information about this woman. He's drifted now from just temptation to action. He's making plans.

Throughout the Leader's Notes you will notice the theme of "sending." This might be a theme you want to develop in your group discussion.

Question 7

In the Old Testament, generally speaking, genealogies don't mention spouses. They might talk about someone's ancestors, but not about a spouse. When a person is mentioned by name, often their father is also listed, but not a spouse. So when the servant mentions the name of Bathsheba's husband, this is a flashing warning light.

If David were at a spiritually sensitive place with God, this statement would have stopped him in his tracks. David, this is someone's wife, someone's daughter. But thinking is the last thing David wants to do. He just hits the accelerator and floors it. He goes right through this crossroads.

In verse 4 David sent messengers to get Bathsheba. There's that word *send* again. This time he's not sending for information. He's sending for the woman, using his power to get what he wants.

Up to this point in the story, everything works the way that David plans: he sees, he wants, he inquires, he finds out, he sends for her, he sleeps with her, and then he sends her home. And then something happens that's not in his script.

"The woman conceived and sent word to David, saying, 'I am pregnant'" (2 Samuel 11:5). There's that word again, only this time David is the sendee, not the sender. He hadn't counted on these results. This always happens with sin.

In regard to answering question 7, you might want to suggest that your small group members think about how God might send these warnings—through a conviction of the heart, another person, circumstances, his Word, or by the voice of the Holy Spirit.

Questions 8–9

Even after Bathsheba becomes pregnant, David still thinks he can control things. He starts sending again. He sends for Joab, his military leader, and the deceit continues and grows. He has Joab send Uriah home for a little R & R. David is going into overdrive now. He is in major cover-up mode.

It is ironic that a foreigner, Uriah the Hittite, is more faithful to God than David. He is more faithful when he is drunk than David is sober. He won't sleep with his wife because the other soldiers are out fighting for the nation and their king. If only Uriah would have played along and cooperated with David's plan. One night in his own bed with his wife and David would be off the hook. When Bathsheba began to look pregnant, Uriah would say, "Hey, that must have happened when I got that weekend leave."

Now we see how far David is willing to go. He sends again. This time he sends a letter to Joab, by the hand of Uriah. The letter is the explanation of how Uriah is to be eliminated, killed, on the battlefield. Of course, it would mean even more soldiers dying so it did not look too suspicious. But David is ready to do whatever is necessary to cover up his sin, no matter the cost.

Finally, the news comes. In a "tragic" battle, Uriah was killed. So, David sends one more time. After a period of appropriate mourning (you would not want to be inappropriate at a time like this), David sends for Bathsheba once again and has her brought to his house. This time she comes to be his wife. He's gotten away with murder and nobody would ever know.

Questions 10–11

In 2 Samuel 12:1, "The LORD sent Nathan to David." Here is that word *sent* one more time, the last instance in this story. Now the Lord sends because when the Lord starts sending, nobody else is going to send anymore. The Lord is the last sender.

David has been playing God with a lot of people's lives for a long time now, probably for over a year because the baby has been born. He's been playing God with Bathsheba and Uriah and Joab and the army and all Israel, like a spider just sitting in the middle of the web. Sin always involves the temptation that Adam and Eve faced in the very beginning: the promise that we can be like God.

When we have blasted past all the crossroads, God will do some sending. In the case of this story, God sends Nathan to David. Nathan must have given a great deal of thought as to how he would approach the king with this message. Nathan has to find some way to get past all of David's defenses and the hardness of his heart. So he thinks, and I'm sure he prays, and finally it's given to him. He will tell David a story. When he does, David is outraged!

In the midst of all his darkness, David is capable of so much self-deception that he says, "As surely as the LORD lives"—he speaks with very spiritual language—"this man deserves to die."

Then comes one of the most courageous statements in Scripture. You can imagine now what's going on inside Nathan. He's standing before the king, not just a friend or a peer. This is King David. And this is not the same David who shepherded little sheep or who defied Goliath. This is a ruthless man. This is a liar, an adulterer, a murderer.

Nathan is risking his life, but he doesn't hesitate. He looks David in the eye and says, "You are the man, David. This is your sin. This is how far you have fallen. This is the depth to which you have descended. This is your heart, your story." Wow!

Then, for who knows how long, there is silence. Surely the thought occurs to David, *I can control this problem too. I took care of Bathsheba, and I took care of Uriah. I took care of Joab, and I took care of the army. And this is just one man, one prophet, one Nathan. I can get rid of him and then I'm home free. No one will ever know. Then I can make up for it and be a good king for the rest of my life.*

But somewhere, somehow, another voice speaks to David—the voice that had whispered to him so long ago when he was just an innocent boy shepherding the sheep; the same voice that had spoken to him back when he was full of idealism and vision, back when he stood against the Philistine giant who had blasphemed his God. Finally, God breaks through and David is broken.

Session Five – A Broken Heart
2 SAMUEL 13–18

Question 1

David's family was messed up. Sometimes we think we invented dysfunctional families in the twentieth century, but this couldn't be further from the truth. Here is a list of the issues David's family faced: adultery, polygamy, substance abuse, years of total estrangement, vandalism, open hatred, rape, murder, and incest. These sins led to broken hearts and deep need for healing and restoration throughout the family system.

Question 2

Notice one thing in the language of this passage which says a lot about the human heart. After Amnon rapes Tamar, he calls his personal servant and demands that she be removed. Take note of how he refers to her, "Get this woman out of here." Amnon can't say "Tamar" or "my sister," but only "this woman."

This is an important theme that runs throughout David's story. Very often, when one person is sinning against another person, they avoid using the person's name or referring to their relationship. It is a way of dehumanizing the person. We saw this in the story of Bathsheba when a servant tried to warn David by saying, "Isn't this Bathsheba? The daughter of Eliam? The wife of Uriah?" In other words, "Isn't this somebody's daughter, somebody's wife, somebody with a name?" But to David she was just "that woman." When Saul was furious with his son, Jonathan, he said to him, "You son of a perverse and rebellious woman," not "my son." We all do this when we're involved in sin against someone. We don't want to think of them as "my brother," "my sister," "my neighbor." It's just "that nameless person."

Questions 4–6

Why didn't David confront Amnon and deal with this horrible situation? Maybe he was preoccupied with being king. Maybe he was afraid of what Amnon might do in response. Parents are like that sometimes. Sometimes parents need to do hard things, say tough words, but they're afraid of what their children will do back and so they don't do anything.

There might also be another reason. Look closely at Amnon's behavior. He lusted after a woman, and then he figured he could use his own power and position to take what he wanted from her and discard her when he was through. Where do you think he might have gotten an idea like that? Where have we heard a sad story like that? David may have been paralyzed by his own fallenness and the guilt of his past sins. Who was he to call someone out for doing the same thing he had done?

In any relational world, especially in a family, when sin is not dealt with directly and redemptively, it leads to more sin. You can take that to the bank. And that's what happens with David and his family.

Questions 7–8

Can you imagine the level of frustration and anger in the heart of Absalom when the only way he knows to get his dad's attention is to set a field on fire? Kids will do that. They would like to have their parents' loving attention, but if they can't get it any other way, they'll "set fields on fire" by using drugs, getting pregnant, breaking laws.

Perhaps when they do those things, it's not just defiant rebellion or foolishness. Sometimes what's really going on is they are desperately hoping that somebody will pay attention to them. And kids aren't the only ones to use this tactic; lots of adults have learned to set their own kinds of subtle fires.

Absalom finally set the ultimate fire ... he took over his father's kingdom. He did it over time and with an intentional strategy. The text says, "Absalom stole the hearts of the people." Since Amnon, the firstborn of David's sons, was out of the way, Absalom saw a clear path to the throne. Oh, there was one little obstacle ... his father David was still on it.

Questions 9–10

When David received the message that Absalom was dead, the writer says that the king was shaken. Shaken, because suddenly he saw so clearly the life that was entrusted to him, the baby that he held in his hands so many years ago. This was the child who adored his father, the little kid that would play soldiers and pretend he was David slaying Goliath. He had wanted to be just like his famous daddy.

David was shaken because he thought of all the things that could have been, but now would never be. He thought of the father that he wanted to be, could have been, but wasn't. He thought of all the stupid choices he made, all the things he should have said to Absalom when he was alive but didn't, and finally he pronounced the one word that he could not bring himself to say all this time.

All of a sudden he says it, and he can't stop saying it. It's as if he's been storing it up all these years: "O my son Absalom! My son, my son Absalom! If only I had died instead of you—Oh Absalom, my son, my son!"(2 Samuel 18:33).

In life we can learn from good examples as well as bad examples. When we see a bad example, as we do in David's life in this session, we should take what he did, turn it upside down, and do the opposite.

Maybe you feel it's too late to restore a broken relationship and heal a broken heart. What we can learn from David is that as long as a human heart beats, there is time for healing and grace and forgiveness.

Session Six — A Generous Heart
I SAMUEL 30; 2 SAMUEL 24

Questions 1–2

Too many Christians are confused and defeated when it comes to living a generous life. "What does the Bible teach about possessions and materialism? Am I supposed to give away everything that I have? Should I feel guilty about owning or enjoying anything?" we wonder.

If we can't find solid biblical answers to these questions, some of us just drift into whatever standards our society deems acceptable. The problem is that the Bible says, "Don't let this world squeeze you into its mold." In our day, there is no area of life where Christians get squeezed into the world's mold more than in the area of material possessions. We have to get a handle on this topic and looking at the life of David is a great place to start.

David did not live like a hermit — and he wasn't called to. Like many in our society, David was entrusted with much in the way of material possessions. He wasn't called to give all of his stuff away. But he was called to make sure it did not get ahold of his heart. Over the years, David developed one of the most generous hearts in Scripture.

Questions 3–5

According to 1 Samuel 30, David was living in the wilderness with those who were in debt, distressed, and discontented. They had established a refugee village in Ziklag. While he and all the men were off fighting battles, Amalekites came and burned down their village, carrying off their wives, their children, and all their possessions.

When David and his men, fatigued from their battles and travels, came home and discovered what had happened, they were angry and felt hopeless. But David rallied them and called them to rise up and pursue the culprits. There were six hundred men, but two hundred were so exhausted that they no strength or spirit to go after the Amalekites. So David had them stay with the supplies.

As David and the men marched off, they came across an Egyptian in the desert. He had been left to die by his master and, at that point, had been without food or water for three days and three nights.

David and his men weren't just strangers; they were Israelites, by nature mortal enemies of the Egyptians after having been enslaved by them for four hundred years. The best this abandoned slave could have expected from them was to be left alone to die in peace. More likely, he could expect to be killed.

This is when David's generous spirit surfaces. David said to this man, "What's mine is yours," and gave him precious water and food to revive him. As David soon discovered, the Egyptian turned out to be a servant of one of the Amalekites who had invaded Ziklag. This man led David and his men to the Amalekites; they overcame them, rescued their families, recovered their goods, and headed home.

Some of the four hundred men who had followed David on this rescue mission declared that the two hundred who were too tired to travel and fight should not get a share of what was recovered. They were willing to let them have their wives and kids, but none of the material things.

To this day, that's the way the world works. Generally when we see people in need, our tendency is to make sure not to do anything that would threaten our fulfillment and security. The secret to fulfillment is basically "more stuff for me and less stuff for others."

But David flipped the tables and determined that everyone —those who went to battle as well as those who stayed with the supplies—should share evenly. What a generous spirit! What an example of looking out for others and not just himself. David was so serious about this that he made it the law of the land. He wanted the four hundred who went into battle to remember that there was a time that all of them were discontented, indebted fugitives. He longed for them to see that God had been gracious and generous to them so that they could be gracious and generous with others.

Questions 6–8

Second Samuel 24 recounts a plague God brought on Israel for David's disobedience. At last God stretched forth his hand to stop the destruction, and Jerusalem was momentarily spared. We pick up the drama in verse 18 as David pursued a piece of land, a threshing floor, so that he might set up an altar and give offerings to God, on both his and the nation's behalf.

As the king, David could have simply taken the land. He had the power to do that. Instead, he offered to pay for it. When Araunah, the owner of the threshing floor, offered it for free, David said, "No." He insisted on paying a good price. His generosity was shining through again. He wanted to be generous toward Araunah and also toward God. David did not want to give an offering to God that cost him nothing.

Questions 9–11

First Chronicles 29 describes how David leads the people in giving gifts for the building of the temple. He wants to build a house for the worship of God and the gathering of God's people, to symbolically express God's presence in their midst. David's generous and joyful example is contagious. The leaders and all the people catch his spirit and the resources come pouring in. They don't feel forced or manipulated. They give willingly, overjoyed to share in God's work.

David and the people are facing a project on a scale they have never experienced before. It could have been overwhelming but David's perspective inspires all the people. He declares, "Everything comes from you, God. What we give to you just comes from your hand. All this abundance is just stuff that you've given to us." David's outlook on material possessions can be captured simply as, "It's not my stuff, God; it's yours."

WILLOW
Willow Creek Association

Willow Creek Association
Vision, Training, Resources for Prevailing Churches

This resource was created to serve you and to help you build a local church that prevails. It is just one of many ministry tools that are part of the Willow Creek Resources® line, published by the Willow Creek Association together with Zondervan.

The Willow Creek Association (WCA) was created in 1992 to serve a rapidly growing number of churches from across the denominational spectrum that are committed to helping unchurched people become fully devoted followers of Christ. Membership in the WCA now numbers over 12,000 Member Churches worldwide from more than ninety denominations.

The Willow Creek Association links like-minded Christian leaders with each other and with strategic vision, training, and resources in order to help them build prevailing churches designed to reach their redemptive potential. Here are some of the ways the WCA does that.

- **The Leadership Summit**—a once a year, two-and-a-half-day conference to envision and equip Christians with leadership gifts and responsibilities. Presented live at Willow Creek as well as via satellite broadcast to over 130 locations across North America, this event is designed to increase the leadership effectiveness of pastors, ministry staff, volunteer church leaders, and Christians in the marketplace.

- **Ministry-Specific Conferences**—throughout each year the WCA hosts a variety of conferences and training events—both at Willow Creek's main campus and offsite, across the U.S., and around the world—targeting church leaders and volunteers in ministry-specific areas such as: small groups, preaching and teaching, the arts, children, students, volunteers, stewardship, etc.

- **Willow Creek Resources®**—provides churches with trusted and field-tested ministry resources in such areas as leadership, evangelism, spiritual formation, spiritual gifts, small groups, stewardship, student ministry, children's ministry, the use of the arts—drama, media, contemporary music—and more.

- **WCA Member Benefits**—includes substantial discounts to WCA training events, a 20 percent discount on all Willow Creek Resources®, *Defining Moments* monthly audio journal for leaders, quarterly *Willow* magazine, access to a Members-Only section on WillowNet, monthly communications, and more. Member Churches also receive special discounts and premier services through WCA's growing number of ministry partners—Select Service Providers—and save an average of $500 annually depending on the level of engagement.

For specific information about WCA conferences, resources, membership, and other ministry services contact:

Willow Creek Association
P.O. Box 3188
Barrington, IL 60011-3188
Phone: 847-570-9812
Fax: 847-765-5046
www.willowcreek.com

Just Walk Across the Room Curriculum Kit
Simple Steps Pointing People to Faith

Bill Hybels with *Ashley Wiersma*

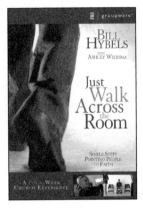

In *Just Walk Across the Room*, Bill Hybels brings personal evangelism into the twenty-first century with a natural and empowering approach modeled after Jesus himself. When Christ "walked" clear across the cosmos more than 2,000 years ago, he had no forced formulas and no memorized script; rather, he came armed only with an offer of redemption for people like us, many of whom were neck-deep in pain of their own making.

This dynamic four-week experience is designed to equip and inspire your entire church to participate in that same pattern of grace-giving by taking simple walks across rooms—leaving your circles of comfort and extending hands of care, compassion, and inclusiveness to people who might need a touch of God's love today.

Expanding on the principles set forth in Hybels' book of the same name, *Just Walk Across the Room* consists of three integrated components:

- Sermons, an implementation guide, and church promotional materials provided on CD-ROM to address the church as a whole
- Small group DVD and a participant's guide to enable people to work through the material in small, connected circles of community
- The book *Just Walk Across the Room* to allow participants to think through the concepts individually

Mixed Media Set: 978-0-310-27172-7

Pick up a copy at your favorite bookstore!

ZONDERVAN®
.com

When the Game Is Over, It All Goes Back in the Box DVD

Six Sessions on Living Life in the Light of Eternity

John Ortberg with *Stephen* and *Amanda Sorenson*

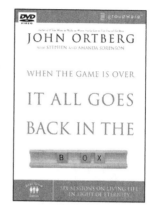

Using his humor and his genius for storytelling, John Ortberg helps you focus on the real rules of the game of life and how to set your priorities. *When the Game Is Over, It All Goes Back in the Box DVD* and participant's guide help explain how, left to our own devices, we tend to seek out worldly things, mistakenly thinking they will bring us fulfillment. But everything on Earth belongs to God. Everything we "own" is just on loan. And what pleases God is often 180 degrees from what we may think is important.

In the six sessions you will learn how to:

- Live passionately and boldly
- Learn how to be active players in the game that pleases God
- Find your true mission and offer your best
- Fill each square on the board with what matters most
- Seek the richness of being instead of the richness of having

You can't beat the house, notes Ortberg. We're playing our game of life on a giant board called a calendar. Time will always run out, so it's a good thing to live a life that delights your Creator. When everything goes back in the box, you'll have made what is temporary a servant to what is eternal, and you'll leave this life knowing you've achieved the only victory that matters.

This DVD includes a 32-page leader's guide and is designed to be used with the *When the Game Is Over, It All Goes Back in the Box* participant's guide, which is available separately.

DVD-ROM: 978-0-310-28247-1
Participant's Guide: 978-0-310-28246-4

Pick up a copy at your favorite bookstore!

The Case for Christ DVD

A Six-Session Investigation of the Evidence for Jesus

Lee Strobel and *Garry Poole*

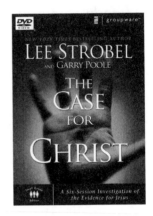

Is there credible evidence that Jesus of Nazareth really is the Son of God?

Retracing his own spiritual journey from atheism to faith, Lee Strobel, former legal editor of the *Chicago Tribune*, cross-examines several experts with doctorates from schools like Cambridge, Princeton, and Brandeis who are recognized authorities in their own fields.

Strobel challenges them with questions like:

- How reliable is the New Testament?
- Does evidence for Jesus exist outside the Bible?
- Is there any reason to believe the resurrection was an actual event?

Strobel's tough, point-blank questions make this six-session video study a captivating, fast-paced experience. But it's not fiction. It's a riveting quest for the truth about history's most compelling figure.

The six sessions include:

1. The Investigation of a Lifetime
2. Eyewitness Evidence
3. Evidence Outside the Bible
4. Analyzing Jesus
5. Evidence for the Resurrection
6. Reaching the Verdict

6 sessions; 1 DVD with leader's guide, 80 minutes (approximate). *The Case for Christ* participant's guide is available separately.

DVD-ROM: 978-0-310-28280-8
Participant's Guide: 978-0-310-28282-2

The Case for a Creator DVD

A Six-Session Investigation of the Scientific Evidence That Points toward God

Lee Strobel and *Garry Poole*

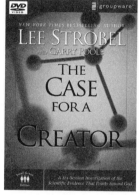

Former journalist and skeptic Lee Strobel has discovered something very interesting about science. Far from being the enemy of faith, science may now provide a solid foundation for believing in God.

Has science finally discovered God? Certainly new discoveries in such scientific disciplines as cosmology, cellular biology, astronomy, physics and DNA research are pointing to the incredible complexity of our universe, a complexity best explained by the existence of a Creator.

Written by Lee Strobel and Garry Poole, this six-session, 80-minute DVD curriculum comes with a companion participant's guide along with a leader's guide. The kit is based on Strobel's book and documentary *The Case for a Creator* and invites participants to encounter a diverse and impressive body of new scientific research that supports the belief in God. Weighty and complex evidence is delivered in a compelling conversational style.

The six sessions include:

1. Science and God
2. Doubts about Darwinism
3. The Evidence of Cosmology
4. The Fine-tuning of the Universe
5. The Evidence of Biochemistry
6. DNA and the Origin of Life

The Case for a Creator participant's guide is available separately.

DVD-ROM: 978-0-310-28283-9
Participant's Guide: 978-0-310-28285-3

The Case for Faith DVD

A Six-Session Investigation of the Toughest Objections to Christianity

Lee Strobel and *Garry Poole*

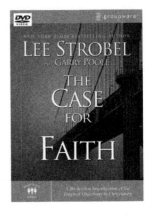

Doubt is familiar territory for Lee Strobel, the former atheist and award-winning author of books for skeptics and Christians. But he believes that faith and reason go hand in hand, and that Christianity is a defensible religion.

In this six-session video curriculum, Strobel uses his journalistic approach to explore the most common emotional obstacles to faith in Christ. These include the natural inclination to wrestle with faith and doubt, the troubling presence of evil and suffering in the world, and the exclusivity of the Christian gospel. They also include this compelling question: Can I doubt and be a Christian?

Through compelling video of personal stories and experts addressing these topics, combined with reflection and interaction, Christians and spiritual seekers will learn how to overcome these obstacles, deepen their spiritual convictions, and find new confidence that Christianity is a reasonable faith.

The Case for Faith participant's guide is available separately.

DVD-ROM: 978-0-310-24116-4
Participant's Guide: 978-0-310-24114-0

Pick up a copy at your favorite bookstore!

ReGroup™

Training Groups to Be Groups

Henry Cloud, Bill Donahue, and *John Townsend*

Whether you're a new or seasoned group leader, or whether your group is well-established or just getting started, the *ReGroup*™ small group DVD and participant's guide will lead you and your group together to a remarkable new closeness and effectiveness. Designed to foster healthy group interaction and facilitate maximum growth, this innovative approach equips both group leaders and members with essential skills and values for creating and sustaining truly life-changing small groups. Created by three group life experts, the two DVDs in this kit include:

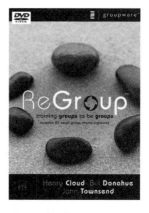

- Four sixty-minute sessions on the foundations of small groups that include teaching by the authors, creative segments, and activities and discussion time
- Thirteen five-minute coaching segments on topics such as active listening, personal sharing, giving and receiving feedback, prayer, calling out the best in others, and more

A participant's guide is sold separately.

DVD: 978-0-310-27783-5
Participant's Guide: 978-0-310-27785-9

Pick up a copy at your favorite bookstore!

No Perfect People Allowed (with 4-Week Church Experience DVD)

Creating a Come as You Are Culture in the Church

John Burke

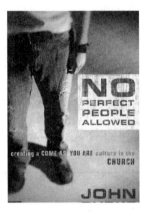

How do we live out the message of Jesus in today's ever-changing culture?

The church is facing its greatest challenge—and its greatest opportunity—in our postmodern, post-Christian world. God is drawing thousands of spiritually curious "imperfect people" to become his church—but how are we doing at welcoming them?

No Perfect People Allowed shows you how to deconstruct the five main barriers standing between emerging generations and your church by creating the right culture. From inspiring stories of real people once far from God, to practical ideas that can be applied by any local church, this book offers a refreshing vision of the potential and power of the body of Christ to transform lives today.

> "We now are living in a post-Christian America—and that means we must be rethinking ministry through a missionary mindset. What makes this book both unique and extremely helpful is that it is filled with real-life stories of post-Christian people becoming followers of Jesus—not just statistics or data about them."
>
> Dan Kimball, Author, *The Emerging Church*

> "... John's 'get it' factor with people, lost or found, is something to behold! Reading this book filled me with optimism regarding the next generation of pastors and faith communities ... "
>
> Bill Hybels, Senior Pastor, Willow Creek Community Church

> "*No Perfect People Allowed* is a timely and necessary word for church leaders in a post-Christian culture. John Burke serves up quite a tasty meal full of the rich nutrients that will strengthen the body of Christ."
>
> Randy Frazee, Senior Minister, Oak Hills Church;
> Author, *The Connecting Church* and *Making Room for Life*

Hardcover, Jacketed: 978-0-310-27807-8

Share Your Thoughts

With the Author: Your comments will be forwarded to the author when you send them to *zauthor@zondervan.com*.

With Zondervan: Submit your review of this book by writing to *zreview@zondervan.com*.

Free Online Resources at
www.zondervan.com/hello

 Zondervan AuthorTracker: Be notified whenever your favorite authors publish new books, go on tour, or post an update about what's happening in their lives.

 Daily Bible Verses and Devotions: Enrich your life with daily Bible verses or devotions that help you start every morning focused on God.

 Free Email Publications: Sign up for newsletters on fiction, Christian living, church ministry, parenting, and more.

 Zondervan Bible Search: Find and compare Bible passages in a variety of translations at www.zondervanbiblesearch.com.

 Other Benefits: Register yourself to receive online benefits like coupons and special offers, or to participate in research.